The Story I Tell Myself

The Story I Tell Myself

HOW SELF NARRATIVES
DEFINE OUR IDENTITY,
HOLD US BACK AND HOW
WE CAN CHANGE THEM

Peter Ash

Peter Ash
http://www.peterwrites.ca/

First Edition Published March 2018

Edited by Mark Swift
Cover design by Paul Dotey (pauldotey.ca)
Photography by Devin Ouelette (devolet.com)

Paperback ISBN 978-1-7752241-1-2
eBook   ISBN 978-1-7752241-0-5

CONTENTS

1

The Story

October 2015. Something was going on with me. The last few months, I'd been feeling good. Confident. Self-assured. It was good, of course, but all a bit uncomfortable. The thing was, I'm not those things. I'm far from confident. I am normally filled with self-doubt, uncertainty, the fear of failure.

But maybe I'm not. I had just realized I've been lying to myself for three decades. I've built, slowly over time, a narrative about who I am for myself. And now something's changed, and that narrative is beginning to crumble.

Me

I started to think and reflect on what was going on. I was starting to see myself differently and it went against who

I had thought I was since I was a kid; it was so confusing and uncomfortable and exciting all at the same time. When I clued in that this was what was happening, I laid out who I had thought I was with words for the first time. This was the story I told myself.

My story went something like this:

I'm a nice guy, but I'm shy. I'm quiet, I'm awkward in social situations, often I'm an outsider, and I have had trouble fitting in, over many years and in many settings. I have suffered from anxiety and because of this I try to avoid a lot of situations and I'm limited in social abilities because of it. I'm smart and aware of the world around me, and I'm probably an interesting person but most people wouldn't "get" me, so I usually don't try to get to know people. I have a few meaningful connections with other people but they are few and far between. I have trouble connecting with others. I don't have many talents, I guess I'm a decent writer, but have no artistic skills, which might make me less interesting/cool/attractive than others who are artistic. I'm sensitive. Caring. But I give up easily, and retreat at the first sign of resistance.

There it was. The story I tell myself. There were many things in there that I wasn't really happy about but it felt familiar.

However, as I was starting to discover, there was a lot in my story that wasn't true, and I started to see that it actually boxed me in in so many ways, and the change I was feeling was what I think was a lot of new growth I was experiencing beginning to battle against that old story. I will break this down in the next chapter so that you can see how I started to unpack this in greater detail.

It was actually a really difficult process to write this out. This story is just something that I knew to be true without having to put words to it. But laying it out like this was actually very powerful. It challenged me to really think about who I was, and once I had this, I was able to start to really understand it, what was true and what wasn't, and see myself in a new way that has led to unbelievable personal growth since.

In short, understanding my self-narrative, my story, has allowed me to reflect and make changes that have been life-altering, and I believe anyone can have similar benefits by looking at their own self-narratives.

What's in a Story

Humans are storytellers. It's a big part of how we communicate. Stories help us give meaning to life, help us understand and share, and form connections with others. We also use them as a way for ourselves to perceive and bring purpose. It had never really occurred to me before that I tell myself a story about my identity, but that essentially, it's true. It's part of how I understand myself and my place in the world. So, what's the big deal about stories?

Well, as much as they help us form our identities, they can also be flawed and close us off to things that are outside the narrative we have for ourselves.

I have realized that there are lots of situations where I wouldn't do something because I had a story that told me I couldn't. Others I know have this, too. From things like weight loss, saving money, public speaking, we can have stories that say, "There's no way I can do that." And then you just don't do it. But these are just stories. It doesn't mean they are true.

Stories are obviously very powerful and can be helpful or harmful. But when it comes to our own self-narratives, we are the storytellers. And as the storytellers, we can change the stories. That's what this book is all about.

Why Me, Why Now?

This journey started for me when a number of things were happening in my life to kick me into this reflective state. My beliefs about myself were being challenged over and over again. I was doing new things at work that challenged my thinking, things I didn't think I could do. Importantly, I was getting feedback from others that countered who I thought I was. I was making new connections with people, experiencing relation-ships differently, and learning new things.

The conditions were right for me to start having these realizations. For you, if you need or want to explore your own self-narrative and how it impacts your life, maybe reading this book will be a shortcut for you and enough to jump-start the process, or maybe you are already thinking about this. Maybe you already have this figured out and none of this will be new to you. No matter where you are at, I hope my own experiences that I am now going to share will at least give you a chance to reflect, which is always a good thing.

Qualified? Who, Me?

I should probably introduce myself and tell you a bit more about me. I am not a psychologist, and have no psychological training. I'm not a celebrity or someone who has lived an exotic lifestyle. To be honest, I'm probably not what most people would consider to be "qualified" to write a self-help book. I'm just someone trying to figure things out, maybe like you.

I'm in my thirties, fully an adult, I guess, but still feel like I'm figuring out who I am and what I want in life. I work in healthcare, have an MBA, have a partner and a cat.

The whole idea that I would write a book is still something I'm surprised by. I've had a lot of self-doubt through the writing of this; even with all of the personal growth I'll be telling you about, the doubt was still there. Who am I to be writing a book?

But what I've realized is *why wouldn't I* write this book? I have so much that I want to share, and this is the way for me to do it. So here we are. Take this book for what it is: the probably unqualified opinion of someone figuring things out, as I share what I've learned and what's worked for me. Keep an open mind and be prepared to reflect, and you never know what will happen.

A Few Notes on Reality

Reality is important, and I want to emphasize a couple of things about it here. First, this is a self-help book. I actually prefer the term "personal development" but hey, here we are, I'm now a self-help author. My intention is not to write an airy, new-agey book or create unrealistic expectations. I believe you can really change your life and create new opportunities for yourself by changing your self-narrative, but you also still need to work towards your goals. Things won't magically happen for you without you doing what it takes to achieve what you want.

Secondly, I understand that not everyone has a level playing field. There are many systemic barriers that exist in our world that can create differing conditions and opportunities (or lack of) for different people. For people of colour, of differing sexual and gender identities, women, different socio-economic backgrounds and many more. Changing your self-narrative won't make these magically disappear. It sucks. Let's be real and know that these things exist. But I believe self-narratives are still a very powerful thing, and we can remove our own barriers that we put up for ourselves, see ourselves differently and hopefully create new opportunities for both ourselves and each other.

Bottom line, we need to be grounded in reality while being open to changing ourselves and seeing ourselves differently. We can change what we control, and what we can control is our own self-narratives. We can change the story we tell ourselves and it can change our lives. With that in mind, I believe everyone can benefit from what is in this book.

What's in This Book

This book explores my own experience of personal growth over the past few years. It's nothing more or nothing less than that.

In the next chapter I'll go in depth into my own self-narrative, examining what was true and what wasn't. I'll look at where our narratives come from, and what some psychological theories around them say.

Then I will share with you what I've learned about all of this over the past few years. I have experienced tremendous personal development through this journey and I have laid out for you my big takeaways, in the hope that sharing them with you will give you some new ways of thinking about yourself and enable you to apply them in your life.

Finally, I'll give you a how-to guide. A process which you can follow to try out what I've done if you are so inclined.

How to Use This Book

I understand that we are all on our own journeys, have our own set of experiences and are at different places in our lives. I know some of what I talk about may not resonate with you, and your experiences may be very different than mine. All I ask is that you keep an open mind, be willing to think about yourself in perhaps a new way and above all be honest with yourself. Our narratives are powerful forces in our lives and convince us of things about who we are. It is important that you are able to set those beliefs aside while you self-reflect to see what the truth actually is. It may be very much in line with your narratives, or it might be vastly different. Just be open to examining this for yourself.

I'll just emphasize this again: this book is not based around psychology or any kind of research methodology. It is simply me sharing with you. My hope is that you can gain some new perspective or think about yourself in new ways. At the very least, if this gives you a chance to reflect on who you are, then I believe this will be worth the 100 pages or so you will invest in reading.

2

The Big Three

Thinking about my own narrative, there are three themes that really seem to have shaped who I am today. There are certainly other components of the narrative, but these three broad themes have influenced every aspect of my life for over twenty-five years, for better or worse. I will explore these three themes here, unpacking what they are, how I think they came to be and how they have affected my life, and will then reflect on if they are true.

This is the process I have been going through over the past few years, looking closely at who I think I am. Through this, I really have learned so much about myself, changed my thinking, and experienced tremendous personal and professional growth. Even if these themes don't resonate with you, I hope this look at the process can be of benefit.

One: The Power of Labels: He's Just Shy

One of the biggest stories I've told myself is about being an introvert. It's not that it isn't true, but more about what that means. Thinking back, a big part of my childhood and teen years I was shy. Or at least I was told I was shy. I'm not entirely sure where that label came from. My best guess is probably that some elementary school teacher told my parents that I was shy because I wasn't connecting with the other kids or spent a lot of time alone. Wherever it came from, it stuck.

The label of "shy" carries a lot of baggage with it. Looking the word up in a thesaurus identifies synonyms such as timid, sheepish, nervous, insecure and unconfident. You get the idea. The label really stayed with me throughout my childhood all the way into my twenties. And to be honest, those synonyms could describe how I viewed myself for many of those years. However, at some point I started to really think about being shy. What does it mean? Am I even actually shy, or is that just some label that was given to me? And could a label like that really have that much power to influence my life and behaviours as I thought it had?

It seemed impossible that I wasn't shy. It was such a part of my identity, of my story. Could it really not be true? In my early twenties, I was challenged on the label for the first time. I can't remember the circumstance exactly, but I mentioned to someone about being shy. I was very confident that I was in fact shy, and all that it meant. They were surprised. They didn't see me as shy, and actually described me as outgoing. I was shocked. There was no way I thought of myself as outgoing. This was the farthest thing from who I was. Wasn't it?

This exact thing happened a few more times in my twenties. Each time, I was surprised that others didn't see me as shy. Each time, I thought a bit more about it, and slowly I started to see things differently. Others saw me as social, engaging, outgoing. Getting this feedback felt uncomfortable. It felt weird. It just didn't fit with who I thought I was. What was that about? Why was I getting this feedback from others that was so far away from how I perceived myself?

Not As It Seems

The first time or two that this happened, I think I ignored it. It was weird, and I didn't understand where the others were coming from, but ultimately, I moved on quickly, continuing to know that I was shy. But the more that this happened, I started to reflect on what was really going on. Could these people, some of whom I knew well and who knew me well, really not understand such a fundamental aspect of my personality? I started to reflect on this more and more, and slowly I came to a different understanding of myself.

People were telling me I was outgoing, social, engaging. Three words I would never have used to describe myself. What did they see in me or my behaviours? I started to notice how I interacted with others in social settings. Normally, it's not something I would think about, the way

I am with friends or in groups, but I really tried to consider my interactions, what I did or didn't do, and people's reactions to how I was with them. It's actually not such an easy thing to do, but it was an interesting and eye-opening experience.

I started to be aware. When I'm with friends, I'm talkative, I'm not afraid to share my opinion or thoughts, and I even make some pretty witty comments and can make people laugh. I'm comfortable engaging with others, in fact I even like it. Sometimes, I think I might even be the most talkative one of the group. I realized I'm... outgoing. What was going on?

Upon reflection, thinking about how I actually interact with people, I'm not shy. I'm an introvert, for sure, but that is not the same thing. This may not seem like a big deal, but the meaning behind the words, and the power it has had over me for nearly three decades, is incredible.

Thinking I was shy actually limited me in many ways. I really thought that I wasn't capable of being social and I resisted putting myself in situations where I thought I might have to be social or interact with others I didn't know well. The label told me that I couldn't connect with others well, and that likely people thought I was strange for not being able to fit in. This stuck with me for years and years. And now I see the label of shy played such a disproportionate role in how I interacted with the world.

But realizing I was able to be social, at least in the right settings with the right people, I started to think about myself in different ways. I can be social and outgoing, and even enjoy it sometimes. At work, I can be an effective presenter and facilitate large groups, and be what I call "on" when I need to. Maybe I wasn't so "weird" after all.

New Label

What does being an introvert mean, then, and why does it fit with me? Thinking about the word introvert, and doing some research, I started to identify more and more with the word introvert and less with shy. While a lot of synonyms for introvert also have negative connotations similar to those associated with shyness, there are a few that I think are more positive and that really resonate. For example, introspective, self-aware, collected. Looking beyond what can be found in a thesaurus to articles on and by introverts opened up other descriptions that really fit.

There has also been some effort recently to try to dispel myths about introverts. The idea that being an introvert is somehow less desirable than being an extrovert is certainly still in our culture, and I feel it regularly, but there seems to be a movement towards appreciating what introverts bring to relationships, including in leadership.

I like alone time to recharge and reflect, but I am perfectly capable of being social, and of getting along well with people. In fact, I've always had a fairly active social life, but I held onto this cognitive dissonance for years because my story was always that I'm shy. Surprising what a label someone gives you can do, but it was incredibly powerful.

So, I'm not shy, I'm an introvert. And this label fits so much better for me. I've embraced this as part of my identity over the past few years in such a positive way. Understanding this part of myself has enabled me to fully use my strengths, such as being reflective and thoughtful, while giving myself what I need to really thrive, like setting aside some alone time during busy days. And I've talked about it with others, too, and have been finding fellow introverts who act as extroverts. We've been able to share strategies for when we need to be "on" and how to recharge when we're busy. It's actually been great to connect with others who understand. I've even talked about being an introvert in a job interview, emphasizing how I understand how I work and what strengths I could bring to the role. It wasn't planned, but it came out in one of the questions and I just went for it and spoke honestly. I got the job.

Baggage

Introversion still carries what I think is a stigma around it. We really do live in an extroverted world, and those that are put on a pedestal in our culture tend to be extroverts. Even leaders who are introverts often talk about how they have to be extroverted to the point that people think they are extroverts in order for them to get ahead.

Maybe this is me being sensitive to the issue from personal experience, but I think that being introverted is frowned upon in our society, and is not seen as the ideal. Even, as I mentioned, the label of being "shy" is given to children in a way that regards the trait as being a problem, something to help them with. While I think this is slowly changing, with some high-profile books and TED talks about the positives of being introverted, overall there's still the idea out there that being extroverted is the ideal. And this cultural trend has an effect. It becomes baggage that is added to understanding who you are and how you interact with the world, and it's not helpful.

Two: Otherness

This is huge. Like, really huge. I have always felt like I didn't fit in, didn't belong. I remember being in kindergarten and feeling like I wasn't like the other kids. I had some normal friendships for that age, whatever friendships mean when you're 5 years old, but there was always something that made me different. Not just being different, but *feeling* different. And it's feeling it that really shaped who I am.

Feeling "other" is how my therapist described this to me five years ago, and the word fits. It's more than just not fitting in, it's being different. And this has levels – many, many levels of feeling other that I have discovered over the years. When I was young, in grade school, I definitely felt something was different. There were tangible things I noticed, like that I wasn't into sports like the other boys were, but it was more than that. It really was a feeling like I didn't really fit in or belong, and perceiving that others thought that way about me, too. Even when I did have friends, there was always something that made me feel like it wasn't quite right.

Thinking back to my childhood, it was lonely. I was an only child, which in itself is fine, but my home life was quiet. I had friends come and go but no one that I would consider I was close to or who I felt completely comfortable with. Most summers I didn't really see many other kids from school, and spent most of my time with my parents or watching daytime TV. I felt very disconnected from any sort of social network.

Into high school, I started to develop more meaningful friendships with a few people, but ultimately still felt like I wasn't like everyone else. But by my early teens, I did have what I thought was the reason; I was gay. Understanding and exploring your sexuality can be a challenging thing for everyone. Growing up in a small town, going to a Catholic high school and confronting your sexual identity that is different from the "norm" is even harder. I definitely had bullies who would call me derogatory names, one who physically abused me a few times. Some people would shout names from passing cars while I walked around my town, not doing anything I thought was particularly "gay". And this all got to me. It made accepting myself so much harder, and also played nicely into my narrative about being shy - it was even more reason for me to not put myself into situations that would draw attention to me.

So, this started to all make sense. I *was* different. I was "other". As terrible as these experiences were, and they were terrible, I started to feel a bit better because at least

I knew there was a reason for all of this. I faced challenges accepting my sexuality but as I worked through it, it was comforting to know this was why I was feeling like I wasn't like everyone else.

But as I moved away for school, found other people "like" me, and made a good group of friends, I still felt something was off. I still wasn't able to fully connect. Maybe being gay wasn't what made me not fit in. Maybe it was just me? When I dealt with my sexuality, I felt sure that when I was older and could find a community of gay people that things would work out, that I would finally feel normal, like I fit in. But when I found that community and still felt like I wasn't the same as everyone else, it was absolutely devastating.

I remember feeling resigned when I came to this realization. I concluded I was weird, a misfit, and that I'd just have to accept that. I had a partner by this time, so I think I thought I could be happy with him but wouldn't be able to have other close relationships. And really, that's the way things went for years. He would maintain social connections, I didn't have a social life outside of what he organized for us, and people only really liked me because I was with him, or that's the self-narrative that developed, anyway.

It has only been through therapy, and exploring this self-narrative that is the content for this book, that I have been able to begin chipping away at this, and realized that this whole being "other" identity isn't really a thing. And the doors and opportunities that have opened up since then have been incredible.

What This Has Done

Feeling like I don't fit in, or like I'm 'other' as my therapist called it, has been a big part of my self-narrative for most of my life. As I mentioned, beginning in early childhood I felt different. This really stuck with me, and started to be part of who I thought I was. I thought that I didn't fit in, that I was different, that I wouldn't get along with people, and in large part I didn't. This impacted my ability to form relationships with people. Whether I was in fact different than others almost didn't matter, because the fact that I felt like this was enough to make me feel like, or rather know, that I couldn't connect with others and have meaningful relationships, friendships or otherwise.

My story about this really conditioned me to feel like this, so my actions reflected this belief. I didn't try to connect with others in any significant way, because I knew that I couldn't. I had some relationships that had developed over time, but the thought of meeting new people and becoming close friends seemed impossible to me. Whenever I met someone new, I remember thinking that there was no way that they would want to get to know me, or that they could understand me, and so I usually made no effort to get to know them. And this felt bad. After finding my partner, I let him make friends for us. I assumed people just really liked him and so were friends with me by association. I lived most of my twenties with this mindset. I had a few select friends, my partner and everyone else that I thought was just friendly to me because of my partner. It didn't feel great.

The other aspect of this was my self-esteem. Of course,

my perceived lack of ability to connect with others because I was different felt pretty bad, but more than that, I hated feeling like I didn't fit in. I felt different and "other", not in a way that made me unique or to be appreciated, but in a way that I regarded myself as weird or not "normal". I walked around for years feeling like this, and in part I think this was responsible for me having constant low self-esteem. Feeling like a weirdo who's unable to connect with other humans doesn't exactly empower you.

Another thing I've realized is that this theme is tied to being an introvert. And like many things in our narratives, the themes are related, and often have a cumulative effect. Being an introvert and needing time to not be social, or appreciating my alone time, fed into the idea that I was unable to connect because I was different. This just reinforced my narrative and over the years made it incredibly strong.

It's crazy for me to think back on this and how much this impacted on me in my past. Right now, I'm a few years on from changing this aspect of my story and it is with this new perspective that I am really able to appreciate how much it had an impact on me. Not only was the effect huge, but it also makes me consider opportunities I didn't take over the years. Friendships that didn't develop, events I didn't go to, or times when I didn't speak up at work, all because my narrative held me back and closed me off from these opportunities. It's immeasurable, and a bit overwhelming to think about. But this clarity that I've developed about if this part of my narrative is really true has been truly life-changing.

The Truth

So, was this part of my story really true? I grew up always thinking I was so different from those around me. And in truth, growing up queer in a small town, at a religious school, I was pretty different than most of the people I knew. But I let this narrative stretch into adulthood, and let it hold me back. Instead, what I've begun to realize is that I'm different than many people in a lot of ways, but I also share numerous similarities with others, too. And even in my differences, it's OK for me to be unlike others, and it doesn't prevent me from making connections. This is the kind of lesson that is taught in kindergarten, but it's taken me until my thirties to fully appreciate this.

There is a comfort in being ok with who you are and what makes you different. Maybe this is what has changed in me – not so much that I'm not different than a lot of the people around me, but that I've realized that it's ok to be different. And, importantly, surrounding myself with people who recognize and appreciate what makes me different. This acceptance isn't easy and has taken years for me, but I think I'm finally getting it.

This change in my narrative has really opened up possibilities for me in many areas of my life. Really it is a pretty life-changing realization. The old story I had about being other prevented me from even imagining I could have close friendships, and I even told myself that my connection with my partner must have been some sort of fluke, or that he was the only one who was able to see past my otherness.

My new narrative allows me to appreciate the ways that I am unlike others. It also lets me see how much I have in common with people, and this is a change of focus that has done a lot for allowing me to connect with others. I have been able to form some close connections with people and feel so much more confident in interacting with people, both personally and professionally.

More than just removing some false barriers I've set up for myself when it comes to interacting with others, recently I've really started to appreciate what makes me different, and even like it. Hopefully this hasn't been an issue for you, but for so many years I thought the things that made me different or weird were negative, but now I see so much more clearly that they are what I can bring to relationships and need to be shared and not hidden.

Even writing this I feel cheesy; this is new-agey, love yourself kind of stuff, but there's no other way to put it. Changing my narrative about being other has changed how I think about myself in relation to the world, and opened up the potential for meaningful connections. Beyond that, I feel much more confident about who I am, and that really does affect every aspect of my life.

Three: Good Enough

When I started therapy about five years ago, one thing that became incredibly clear to me is that a lot of my emotional reactions to situations in my life actually weren't about the issue at hand, at least not really. A lot of my reactions were more about old feelings, things from my childhood that have had a lasting impact for me. Things would come up in life that hit these nerves, and I would have reactions that were powerful and in a lot of cases harmful.

I often struggle with this, as my emotional response to some situations seems to be disproportionate to what the situation calls for logically. While this realization has helped incredibly, I still have a lot of nerves that get hit and have to try to process what is actually happening and what my emotions are really about. It's hard because often I am experiencing such strong emotions that it can be difficult to move past them and try to see what was really going on.

One big one for me is feeling like I'm not good enough. From talking with others and hearing them share their stories, I think this is a common narrative among people. For me, this feeling definitely formed in childhood. I remember always feeling like this, in various settings, with different groups of people and for various reasons. But it's always been there. And, I hate to admit, still is there.

It manifests in diverse ways, without always being clear that this is the nerve that has been hit. Sometimes it makes sense, like having a terrible time with rejection. This is not uncommon, of course – lots of people struggle with this – but it became clear to me that rejection, in its various forms, makes me feel like I'm not good enough, and brings me back to that exact same feeling from my childhood.

Other ways I experience this are a little less direct, like jealousy. Overall, I wouldn't consider myself a jealous person. I've chosen to have some amazing people in my life, and want to see them succeed and thrive. I'm completely confident in my relationship and not jealous with my partner at all. But sometimes, something will trigger a feeling of jealousy in me still, and it can be incredibly crippling. In addition, there is now an added layer of feelings in that I think I'm too old or too mature to feel this way, and almost feeling a sense of shame for having these reactions to situations or people in my life.

Another way this feeling shows itself is through what is often described as the "little voice in my head". You probably know this as well. As you are working on something or thinking about starting a new endeavour, a negative voice comes into your thought process telling you that you can't do it, or that your idea is stupid, or even worse insulting you personally. This negative pattern of thinking, for me at least, ties to this concept of not feeling like I'm good enough, and can cycle downward quite quickly. It's counterproductive, restricting and truly an awful trap that I can get stuck into.

Of course, all of this has affected my professional life as well. Having that self-doubt about not being good enough held me back early in my career. I stayed in positions too long because I didn't think I was capable, or "good enough", for the next level of job. I would stay silent in meetings when I had something to say because I was so afraid of being shot down, or being judged by colleagues. Ultimately, at least early on in my career, it even prevented me from having a career direction. I didn't know what my career goals were because I didn't think I could actually be good enough to do anything more significant than what I was already doing. In hindsight, this seems silly, sad even. But that's the power of our self-narratives – they really can prevent us from being everything we are capable of, or even having a vision for where we want to go.

Pervasive

This seems to be the hardest part of my story to change. It is incredibly widespread, seemingly affecting any aspect of my life and having a role to play in different scenarios. It can creep up anywhere at any time, even when I least expect it. It even creeps up when things are going really well, and there is no reason to have this way of thinking.

Situations in life come up that present opportunities for these feelings to return, or for that voice to start doing its thing. Rejection is a giant platform for these feelings to happen on, and it's easy to jump to feeling like I'm not good enough, even if the reality might involve other factors. Jealousy can creep up and make me feel like others are better than me for whatever reason. Starting a new project or an idea can bring up the self-doubt that is associated with not being good enough - this book project is an example of that, where I struggled with not thinking I was good enough to write a book, or that I don't have the knowledge to make something people would want to read.

This really seems to be an underlying part of my self-narrative that manifests itself in many different ways. In some aspects, it seems more pervasive than all the other parts of my narrative, like being an introvert, because it can creep up in unrelated parts of my life, in unexpected ways. While being an introvert, or thinking that I'm shy, has me expecting to encounter challenges or be held back in social situations, for instance, this feeling of not being good enough can emerge in any part of any aspect of my life. Socially, romantically, in work, during creative projects. It can be all-encompassing. I think all of this makes it the part of my pre-existing narrative that is the hardest challenge to shift.

Validation

What I am coming to realize is that when I feel like I'm not good enough for something, I'm craving some form of external validation. I'm waiting for someone to tell me that in fact I am good enough, or that what I did was good. This external validation I think comes from my own insecurities and lack of confidence in myself. Having someone tell me something positive gives me a boost, albeit mostly a short-term one, and can keep me motivated. In the absence of that, and in the presence of insecurities, creeps up this feeling that I don't have what it takes, or what I'm doing won't be sufficient. Thankfully this isn't a constant feeling, but when the conditions are right it happens, and it does happen more than I'd like.

The need for validation, to confirm my worthiness, is complex. The root cause, like most of my other challenges and parts of my narrative, is from my childhood. I'm not entirely sure of the conditions that made this an issue for me, although it's related to being other as I previously explored. Thinking about how I can address this, I realized I need to stop looking for external validation. What will fix this challenge is looking within, and having myself be the one who determines if I'm good enough. This sounds simple but is hard as it goes against decades of searching for someone else to tell me that I'm OK.

This is something I'm still working on and it will take time to change, but as with anything, awareness and acknowledgement is the first step. Consciously reminding myself that it's not about anyone else, it's about me, is all I can do to start to change my thinking. It's starting to work, but will take more effort. You can't undo years of thinking overnight, but keeping this perspective is helping. If this is something you struggle with, see if the above fits with you, this need for external validation, and try thinking differently about it, and looking within. Perhaps it can start to shift your thinking as well.

The Truth

So, what's the truth? As I mentioned, this is the hardest part of my story to shake. Having said that, I have had some realizations about this that are helping me handle this narrative as it comes up in various parts of my life.

Recognizing that this informs various reactions and emotions that I have throughout my life has been helpful. Knowing that my feelings in some circumstances are not really about the specific situations at hand, but can actually tie back to this old feeling of not being good enough, has been helpful in allowing me to process my emotions more effectively.

Additionally, I've come to learn that being good enough should not be about receiving validation from others. It should be you who defines if you are good enough. This has been really hard for me to come to terms with, as often I do crave external validation, and when I get it, it seems like an instant fix. But those fixes are often just Band-Aids, and fade away quickly before I need more. What I really need to be looking for is if I am happy with what I'm doing, where I am in my life, and who I am as a person.

And when it comes down to it, things like being good enough are subjective. Focusing inwards, and developing a strong sense of who I am and what I want, will help me figure that out.

Am I good enough? That's up for me to determine, and I need to let go of feelings from my childhood about not being good enough, as they just aren't relevant. Not relying on others for validation is harder than it seems, but it's worth making yourself less reliant on others to feel like you are good enough. It's just important to remember that as long as you are comfortable with who you are, then in those moments where emotions around things creep up, it really doesn't matter what others think.

3

Origin Story

All this reflection took me back to some of my earliest memories, remembering experiences that had an impact on my self-narrative. It made me realize just what an impact events from our past have in shaping who we are in the present, and ultimately our future selves as well.

Thinking about this, I started to recognize my self-narrative was created and developed by these events and situations from my past. My next thought was around what actually creates our self-narratives; what is their origin and why do they come to be?

I thought through what I had learned by identifying my story and tried to think where it all came from. I identified a few key things about my self-narrative that really ring true for me.

Childhood

My self-narrative formed from early childhood into my teens. Basically, all the crap that I'm dealing with internally can be traced back in some way to this period of my life and the events or situations that occurred around then.

It's not that my experiences as an adult don't influence or shape who I am. Of course they do, and it's the experiences that I've had over the past few years that have brought me to these realizations that I'm now discussing here. But thinking through those parts of my narrative that I am struggling with today, they all stem from when I was growing up.

Basically, my theory is that what happens to us in our childhood sets us up for what issues we will have to deal with for the rest of our lives. Our past can really mess us up for life.

The good news, though, as I will explore in later chapters, is that through self-awareness and some reflection and hard work, we can overcome what limitations our past has created for us. I believe this to be true, and I'll share with you what I did to start to remove those hangovers from another time.

Two Influencers

So, my self-narrative was formed when I was a child and teen. I started to think through what were those instances or experiences that had a role in shaping my narrative. To me, it seemed there were two types of influencers, the greater environment that I was living in, and then specific experiences that happened to me.

Environment

The environment that we exist in plays a huge role in shaping who we are. Thinking about the origins of my self-narrative, part of what really shaped it in my childhood was where I lived.

I grew up in a small, conservative town which had limited examples of diversity, in any of its forms. While my parents were more socially liberal (thankfully!), my day-to-day experiences at school or in the community were shaped by small-town conservative values.

This shaped my narrative, as growing up knowing I was different, I never felt that I really fit in. I had no examples to look up to of people that were different and were celebrated for their differences. My feeling of "otherness" started here. Beyond being different in my sexuality, as I started to form my values, I saw they were dissimilar to those of a lot of people I would interact with, further making me feel isolated.

The wider culture also played a role. I was a kid in the '90s, knowing I was different than everyone else at age 5 or 6, realizing I was probably gay around age 11. What I saw in the media in terms of gay representation was gay guys being made fun of or being the centre of jokes, and that they would supposedly all contract AIDS and die a horrible death. In short, there was nothing positive to look forward to in my life as I came to terms with my sexuality.

This all just reinforced what I was seeing in my own town in my day-to-day life.

Thinking back, I was very lonely as a kid. This loneliness, isolation, feeling of otherness and difference, and lack of finding acceptance, informed who I became. These feelings lingered well into adulthood, even when they weren't true or relevant anymore. Finding friends, acceptance and people that were celebrated for their differences was great, but those feelings from my younger self were still there influencing how I viewed myself.

Experiences

The environment played a big factor in shaping who I was, but of course individual experiences shaped my narrative even further. There are so many that made my story be what it was, but to share an example, a lot centred on being bullied as a kid.

As I detailed, I was different than the other kids, and didn't really fit in. Anyone who's different as a kid is a prime target for bullies. And I was a target. I remember switching schools when I was 11, and going to a new school when you don't know anyone is a trying experience even for the most well-adjusted and popular kids, let alone someone who isn't like everyone else.

At the new school, I stood out and there were those who took advantage of that. Surprisingly, my memories of this are that kids a year or two older than me were the ones who really picked on me, and not so much those my own age. Regardless, recess and lunches were torture. I tried to find excuses to stay inside, or just hid by the doors until the bell rang.

There was lots of name-calling, especially around being gay. I was just figuring this all out for myself, and certainly didn't want to draw attention to it. It's amazing that others could see this and bug me about it before I was able to fully process it myself. It sucked.

Even into high school, as I did make some friends and started to figure out who I was a bit more, there were those at my school that would call me names, and who even got physical. I was fortunate not to ever have been "beaten up" but it was common that I would get shoved in the hall, pushed around, spat on.

There was one instance that really sticks out in my memory. I was walking on the main street of my town with a friend, and one of my main bullies was walking towards us. He spewed the usual names as he got close, but when he got to us he stopped, and shoved me hard into a phone booth. I wasn't seriously hurt but I was terrified.

More than the physical fear, I was most upset about being embarrassed in front of my friend. I was so ashamed. Things like this made me feel awful about who I was, and all I could see when I thought about the future was that this would just continue.

The result of all of this was that I was fearful of attention, wanted to blend in as much as I could, and was terrified someone would notice me being different and say something in front of others. I believe these experiences reinforced my story of otherness and not fitting in, as well as my low self-worth.

There are of course lots of other experiences that happened and shaped who I was, but the above will hopefully give you an idea of ways in which our experiences when we are younger can shape our narratives.

The Importance of Origins

For me, it was important to explore the origin of my self-narrative to really understand what it was all about. Later on, I will explore how I looked at what my self-narrative was telling me, and how it influences my actions, behaviours and responses to situations that occur in my life. Thinking through the origin of your self-narrative is part of the process of self-awareness that I'll cover in later chapters.

4

So What?

We're a few chapters in, and so far I've told you about my self-narrative, the story that I told myself about who and what I am. I've shared some of my innermost feelings about who I am as a person. I've also shared how that story wasn't really the truth, and how it has held me back in a number of ways.

You might be thinking that's all fine and good, but SO WHAT? I get it, and I'll explain why I think this is all so important and can help you.

I'll start by acknowledging that my narrative and the themes I've gone through may not resonate with you. Maybe you aren't "shy" or an introvert. Maybe connecting with others isn't something you have ever struggled with. Fair; we all have different skills, experiences and challenges, and I don't pretend to know what yours are.

But the value I hope to give you in walking you through

my experience is to show an approach of how you can look at your own narratives, what kind of learnings to look out for, and to maybe get you to think of things in a new and helpful way.

We all have self-narratives, stories that we tell ourselves. You do, your best friend does, your mom does. It's part of what makes us human.

These narratives form over many years, as I discussed in the last chapter, starting in childhood based on our experiences. Even little things that happen to us can shape what these stories we have about ourselves are.

So What? #1

The big "So What?" is that these narratives are always with us, shaping who we are, what we do, how we respond to situations, what we try to achieve in our lives. This is huge!

Often, we are unaware or not conscious of them. We assume we can't do certain things, so we don't even try. Our narrative can hold us back from expanding our view to new opportunities. They shape how we interact with others, impact what goals we set or don't set for ourselves, and influence how we perceive the world around us.

Because of this, it can be truly transformational to look and really understand what our self-narratives are telling us.

So What? #2

The other big "So What?" is that, I believe, by under-standing these narratives we can work on changing them.

And these changes in our narratives open up some opportunities for us that we never would have thought would have been possible. If you think about it, this is really powerful stuff. It's almost like this could be a key to unlocking new, exciting things for us. This has been my experience, and it has been true for me.

I've heard people talk about being defined by their past. In a way, this is demonstrating a lot of self-awareness. They are recognizing that events or experiences from an earlier time have helped define who they are. What I think this is really getting at is the self-narrative. Our past is where our narrative was established, and it is telling us who and what we are, and impacting, or defining, who we are in the present. The next step to this is to not be defined by it.

To do this, we need to really understand what they are, how they are impacting us and identify what we want to change.

What Next?

This, of course, isn't rocket science; we have a narrative that tells us about who we are and themes emerge. But what I was hoping to illustrate by sharing my "themes" is that our stories really have a profound effect on who we are and how we go through our lives. And if stories have an impact on how we live our lives, changing our stories can have an effect on our lives.

I started to realize this and have seen it actually work. Because of how intricately our stories we tell ourselves are linked to our daily lives, I believe it really is an important concept to understand. The "So What" is that understanding our self-narratives helps us understand who we are, and we can to a large extent change these narratives to affect our lives.

This has been my experience. I've learned a lot about myself and have been able to change my narrative and truly change my life. The later chapters of this book will talk to you about the process I went through, and the learnings that I've had.

5

Psychological Theories of Narratives

This book is a way for me to share my own experience and what I've learned over the past few years. But this is really all about my own experience. After exploring this myself, I wanted to look to see what the field of psychology says about self-narratives. I wanted to validate that some of what I've learned is legitimate, and also to further expand my perspective.

I understand this isn't the most exciting stuff for some of us, but bear with me. Within the knowledge that has been built up by researchers, there are some incredibly profound learnings, and I've done my best to summarize what I took away from what I've found.

There is an entire field of research that digs deep into these theories around narratives, and I don't intend to do them justice here. All I want to do is give some background to show that there are some others thinking and learning about this, and to give you a high-level look at what I've learned from looking into them.

Without having a background in psychology, I didn't really know where to start, so I just started googling, and ended up where any good research project starts - Wikipedia. And to be honest, it's a pretty good place to begin.

Narrative Identity

The first psychological theory related to what I was looking at was *narrative identity*, which seems to fit to some degree with what I'm talking about in this book. In fact, reading the first paragraph on its Wikipedia page just made so much sense. It talks about how our experiences are internalized and that we turn those into a story of our lives, of who we are.

Of course, I needed to move beyond Wikipedia to try to really understand more about these concepts. I found the work of Dan P. McAdams, who has really delved into the topic, and has written several papers and publications that explore it in more depth. If you are interested in the psychology behind this, then I recommend looking into his work. I will summarize here what I've garnered from his work.

Specifically, in his 2013 paper *Narrative Identity*, he and his co-author Kate C. McLean outline that a person's "life story" takes our memories and goals and creates our identity. This helps us understand who we are, and also communicate about ourselves to others.[1]

---

1 *Narrative Identity*, Dan P. McAdams and Kate C. McLean, 2013

The paper discusses narrative identity formation as something that emerges in late adolescence. Citing earlier research, the authors discuss that this is when narratives tend to make links from past events to current events. Interestingly, McAdams and his co-author also discuss the idea about how our narrative identities are used in how we process and experience suffering and negative experiences in our lives. Those that demonstrate the ability to process these events through self-exploration and incorporate them into their own stories had better outcomes in many measures of psychological health. In the research, people who were able to detail thoughtful and comprehensive narratives around those experiences (storytelling about themselves) were actually able to demonstrate a clear link to learning, growth and positive personal transformation.

This indicates to me that the way we process our experiences into our own narrative stories has a direct outcome on our lives, and that our narratives – based on our past experiences – actually shape our current experiences and how we process them.

Some other research I found talks about how although our narrative identities are formed by late adolescence, based around experiences in our childhood and teenage years, they are not static. Our narratives can change as we move through our lives, as we encounter new experiences and major life events, and incorporate these into our existing lifelong narrative.[2]

This was validating for me to read. My own experience is that I have been able to shift my narrative, so under-

2 *The Emergence of Narrative Identity*, Kate McLean, 2008

standing that there is research to suggest that our narratives are not locked in from adolescence was reassuring.

One reason I am drawn to this concept of narrative identity and the research that others have done with it is that it also talks to the fact that we as humans are storytellers. We have always told stories, for thousands of years. From cave drawings and oral traditions, to modern forms of art like literature, theatre and film and TV, we communicate messages and meanings to each other through stories. The same is true for ourselves. We naturally create stories about who we are, and use these to help people understand us and give ourselves meaning.

Ideas of Self

Ideas of self are one of the earliest concepts to be contemplated in psychology. Based on my surface-level look, the modern body of research starts with Freud in the 1920s, but the one early theorist that grabbed my attention was George H. Mead. He identified the concept of one's self to be one that is informed and shaped by our environments and our experiences. He discusses self image as a major component of one's view of self.[3]

For me, this actually fits well into what I am beginning to understand about self-narratives. That our experiences, our environment, the people we interact with, all shape our ideas of self.

Going back to McAdams, thinking about the idea of the "self", he explored the concepts of "I" and "Me". He

---

3 *What is the Self and How is it Formed?*, Simon Moesgaard, 2013

describes the "I" as the one telling our own stories, writing our autobiographies, and the "Me" as the star of those stories. The "I" is our self, and the "Me" is itself.[4]

A bit abstract, but what I think I take away from it is that the "I" is who we really are, and the "Me" is who the "I" thinks it is. The "I" creates the "Me", and this impacts how we keep ourselves in check, set goals for ourselves and respond to situations. The point is we create the "me", the person who we think we are, *WE ARE THE AUTHORS* of our own stories. Once we realize this, we can change what our stories say about who we are.

Five Personality Traits

A concept that kept coming up when I was looking for topics on self-identity was the Five Factor Model of Personality, or what is often called "The Big Five". This originated in research done initially during the early 20th century, and seems to have been accepted over the last thirty years as a way to understand differences in personality.[5]

The factors are:

1. Openness to experience,
2. Conscientiousness,
3. Extraversion,
4. Agreeableness and
5. Neuroticism,

forming the acronym OCEAN.

---

4 *The Psychological Self as Actor, Agent and Author*, Dan McAdams, 2013

5 *The Big Five Personality Theory: The 5 Factor Model Explained*, Courtney Ackerman, 2017

Without going into detail on each of these points, these five factors encompass major personality traits, and where we are within each factor helps determine what our personality is. Each has a range, for example Extraversion – you may be more extroverted or introverted.

As my own experience has shown, even though you may fall on one side of these scales, this is just your preferred personality trait, or your tendencies. It does not mean you can't operate outside that. As I identified in the previous chapters, I am very much an introvert but can be extroverted in many circumstances and situations. My point here is don't let your ratings on these scales inform your story to such an extent that you can't work outside your preferred tendencies – you most certainly can!

Personality traits are often seen as more stable or fixed throughout our lives. An introvert isn't going to change into a total extrovert as their primary personality tendency, for example. However, there is some newer thinking on the role of personality traits that suggests they can actually shift with certain interventions, such as cognitive behavioural therapy. A recent meta-analysis identified that personality traits can change due to psychological interventions. Specifically, the personality trait of neuroticism showed potential dramatic change, whereas the others were less moved, with openness being the most resistant to change.[6]

What this shows me is that we really can change many aspects of ourselves. We are not stuck with our traits and narratives, and we can make changes if we want to. This

---

[6] Supplemental Material for A Systemic Review of Personality Trait Change Through Intervention, Brent Roberts et al, 2017

is such a powerful realization, and one that I believe is truly exciting.

So how do personality traits link to narratives? From what I understand and as I mentioned, personality traits tend to be stable and stick with us through our lifetime. That doesn't mean we can't work outside of our preferred traits or that we can't even shift them a bit with various interventions, but they seem to a large degree to be hard-wired through our lives. Our self-narratives are created as we grow up influenced by our experiences and our environments. While they often are formed by late adolescence, they can be changed by new experiences or, as I'm going to show you in later chapters, through deliberate self-reflection and work. Both personality traits and our self-narratives inform us of who we are as a person, and both are crucial for forming our identities.

Both, I believe, influence our behaviour and responses. Our self-narrative is a big part of this, as I'm trying to show with this work, but our personality traits also play an important role. Understanding both will help you have a deep understanding of yourself, and help you as you try to make changes in your life.

If you would like to learn more about the Big Five, I encourage you to search. There are lots of resources including free online tests where you can determine your own personality traits.

Takeaways

This was a really high-level look at some psychology behind what this book is about, so please do look into this more if you are at all interested in any of these topics; there is a lot out there.

For me, researching this was a bit overwhelming, as I have no psychological background and didn't know what I was looking for. But it was also validating in that I know that what I have experienced and think that what I have learned is actually real, and others have researched the concepts I was experiencing and using. It also opened my eyes a bit to how personality and identity are so complex, with many factors influencing them. Understanding these more will only help us learn and grow.

Now, moving on from this, the next chapter will focus on what I've learned from my own experiences.

6

What I've Learned

Now you know more about me and what brought me to this point in my life, I'm going to share what I've uncovered through the past few years. Although you may or may not associate with the specific themes I identified, there are a number of things I've learned about how self-narratives can affect us. I've thought a lot about these over the past couple of years, trying to pull out the meaningful concepts of what I've learned, and what really feels true to me.

This is the start of the "meat" of this book, these are the key concepts I'd like to share. I'd like to emphasize again that I'm not a psychologist, I don't have formal training in this area, but these learnings have really helped me in my own development over the past couple of years in ways that I couldn't even imagine when I began exploring this. This is what I'd like you to think through and see if any of it fits with your own situation.

A Challenge

I want to start with emphasizing that this process is not an easy one. It can be hard to fully understand what your story really is. It is often so unconscious and such a part of us that it is hard to pull apart and examine each part of it in detail. It is also uncomfortable to look at aspects of your story that are not the most positive. You might have to face things that you don't want to or that you have been hiding away over the years. But this process of self-reflection is really powerful once you get into it, and you will potentially discover new things about yourself and find new ways of thinking about who you are. It is worth it.

The Voice in My Head

We often hear people talk about the voice in their head. We all have this, and it can give us both positive, reinforcing messages, and negative, detracting ones. One of the first parts of this process for me was to stop and listen to what the voice in my head was saying. Literally stopping and really hearing what it was saying. This is something I never really thought about before; I would just blindly hear whatever it was telling me without much thought.

I'm not sure what this voice really is, but for me it has been tied to my narrative. It's a way of my narrative manifesting itself and one of the major ways it influences me. It is sometimes positive. I've been able to calm myself down by having a reassuring voice tell me to chill out in some panicked situations. But often, and most of the time that I notice it, the voice is a nagging presence, reminding me that I'm not good enough, that others don't get me, that I'm doing the wrong thing. I started to realize that this is the kind of message that voice was most often saying. This is not a voice that can ever be useful.

Now that I've changed my narrative, this voice has been turned down. I can't say that it isn't still there, but the volume is so much lower, low enough that another voice can come through - a more positive voice that is helpful and aligned with my new narrative.

Unexamined Assumptions

Another aspect of this process of self-reflection has been that realization that I had many unexamined assumptions about myself. These are aspects of my story that just were, and seemed like they were always there. I never actually examined them in more detail to see if they were true. It never even occurred to me to think about them. Often these are the things that my inner voice is saying.

As I explored earlier in this book, things like being shy or feeling like I wasn't capable of connecting with others were parts of my story. They were there for years, and I never thought to challenge them to see if they were in fact true. Only through this journey that I started in my thirties did I really start to challenge some of these.

There are lots of reasons why we don't think about these things. For instance, if we're not even conscious of them, we don't examine them. I also think that for me they became so consistent that part of me started to believe them, at least to the point that I would no longer question them.

I suspect that all of us have these unexamined assumptions. Are there things about who you are that you have just always accepted to be true? Maybe they are true; I'm not suggesting that everything in your self-narrative is inaccurate, it almost certainly contains many truths. But I do think it is a good exercise to think about these assumptions and challenge them. See what you find, you may be surprised.

Stereotypes

One reflection I had was around stereotypes, and it speaks to our unexamined assumptions. As we develop our stories throughout childhood and adolescence, I also think we can identify with specific stereotypes based on our narratives. If your story is that you are smart, awkward, don't make friends easily, like to read and are introverted, perhaps you gravitated to the idea of being a nerd. The same if you are a jock - you play sports, don't do as well academically, get the girl/guy etc., or whatever broad category you identify with.

Stereotypes are of course generalizations of types of people, and are often used in harmful or unpleasant ways. But they do have an influence on us, and if we identify even slightly with a specific one, it can be a way in which society tells us how we should be. Seeing those stereotypes being portrayed in the media can help inform how we think we should be. This can be a vicious cycle, reinforcing our beliefs about ourselves.

External Validation

I've learned a lot about my need for external validation, and how that ties into my own self-narrative. In a lot of ways, the theme around being good enough is really tied to this. Having someone else give me positive feedback can give me motivation, keep me going, or even turn around a bad mood.

With social media this is even more acute - getting likes on a selfie gives me a boost, a brief high. In some ways, external validation is actually pretty helpful. There have been times when I'm unsure about something I'm working on, and getting positive feedback gives me a different, useful perspective that can confirm the direction I'm going in, or give me something else to think about. In fact, the reason this book came about is largely because of positive feedback I got from writing my personal essays that I originally shared on social media. This external validation was the push that I needed to keep writing and start this book project.

However, there are lots of ways in which external validation can be problematic. Specifically, when it is needed to make you feel good about yourself or to allow you to continue doing the work that you want to accomplish. There is a danger to all of this, in that when you rely on external validation too much, if it then becomes absent it can be crushing. Despite everything else that might be going well, if you don't get that positive feedback, those likes on social media, the invitations to events, you may find nothing can make you happy and end up being down and demotivated.

The need for validation can be – and is for me in my situation – tied to our narratives in some ways. Shifting our narrative can be beneficial and reduce our reliance on others to tell us we're doing ok. If you depend too much on others for this validation, you will struggle to move forward when it's not there. Instead, I've learned I need to be looking inwards for that validation and keep going with what drives me. Let's just say this is a work in progress for me, but it's one of my most life-changing realizations.

External validation is nice, it's a bonus, but it should not be why you do what you do. And it shouldn't be a barrier for you to accomplish your goals.

Root Cause

Now on to some really tough stuff. One of the most help-ful realizations for me that has given me something tan-gible and actionable in my day-to-day life is around root cause.

I actually learned about the concept of root cause in my professional life. Working in healthcare, I was involved in training our staff on quality improvement - basically trying to make things better in their work. A key concept is to stop and understand what the problem or issue really is about, and not jumping to solutions. The idea is that often things occur that are symptoms of something deeper, and if you don't address that root cause, symptoms will keep occurring. I realized the same is true for my emotions, and that I could apply this theory in my personal life.

Here's what I figured out and what was true for me. Things that happen in our lives are often not about what is happening in that situation. They are often tied to things from our past. We talk about "hitting a nerve" when something has a huge emotional effect. I think what's really happening here, at least for me, is often that it's touching on part of our stories that we're not dealing with.

Emotions and reactions that I personally have can be part of this for me. These are the symptoms of the root cause. When I started to understand this and to look for those causes, I was able to handle my emotions much better. They don't go away, and often I will still have those emotional responses to situations that I always had in the past, but now I understand them much better and am able to think through them, making things much easier in those moments.

Beyond Ourselves

Our narratives impact not only on how we view ourselves, but how we interact with the world, including our relationships with others. In addition to the need for external validation, my narrative influenced how I was in social situations and with friends. For years, I didn't think I could connect with others, for a number of reasons that I explored earlier in this book. Because of that narrative I had, I didn't even try. Looking back, there were so many opportunities I missed to become closer to others, or to share experiences with them that I closed myself off to. That has changed as I've changed my narrative.

Failure

An interesting learning I've had is around failure. Failure is something that we don't like to talk about, and we often don't hear others discuss their own failures, as society tends to frown on failures and hide them away and only highlight success. The thing is, we all fail. Hopefully we don't have many large failures in our lives, but we most certainly have many small failures. Things often don't work out as we plan; this happens to everyone. We all have failures in our lives.

You might be wondering, what's the connection of our failures to our self-narratives? For me, as I went through this period of self-reflection and trying to understand and re-write my narrative, I found that even those small failures could really trip me up. They would push me back to my old version of myself that I was trying to get away from, and make me feel like I couldn't change my narrative. Really, even the smallest things could set me back and discourage me. And, of course, the fear of failure is something that has a tremendous ability to make us not want to try new things or grow.

So, what's my big learning? For me, I really had to focus on moving through failures, big and small. Failures don't mean you aren't good enough, or that you can't change. Instead, they offer a great opportunity for you to learn and grow, and by recognizing that you can re-frame your thinking and not let them get in your way. Don't be afraid of failure. Embrace it and learn from it. But most importantly, don't let it discourage you as you try to re-write your narrative.

Like a Bad Habit

Something that I initially found hard to believe is that there is something comfortable about our stories. We know them well, even if we aren't consciously aware of them and how they influence our lives. I realized this because it became increasingly uncomfortable as I tried to change my narrative.

As much as I wanted to change and try to think differently about myself and explore new possibilities, it often felt uneasy, even unnatural. Reverting back to the old story was easy and felt good in some way, despite it being counter to what I was consciously trying to change. In a way, we're addicted to our stories even if they are unhelpful. And like any addiction, they can be hard to break.

Not Just Me

I'll close this chapter with what I found to be a reassuring realization: It wasn't just me that has a story, and I am not the only one whose story is holding them back in different ways. Of course, it makes sense that I'm not the only one who has a self-narrative, but it really isn't something that I had thought about before, and especially not about the influence others' self-narratives would have on our relationships.

Through thinking about those people in my life that I know well, I started to identify patterns of behaviour in people, and even some things that they would say gave some insight into their own narratives of themselves.

Often this would happen after an interaction, as I was reflecting on something they would say about their situations or circumstances that they weren't happy about. Things like "It figures this would happen to me" or negativity about their job or weight or debt, making the same complaints time after time. It gave me insight into how their stories might be holding them back. Of course, as an outsider I only have one perspective, and I was able to talk to some others about their stories and explore this a bit with them. This actually gave me even more insight into my own understanding of myself to see how others' narratives affected them.

It also got me thinking about how our own self-narratives impact our social interactions and relationships. Not only does my narrative have an effect on how I interact with others, but it actually has shaped who I have relationships with. Of course, things like shared values and interests are a major influencer on who we have in our lives as friends or partners, but I also think that our self-narratives play a role.

The company we keep can be a reinforcer of our self-narratives. Often, I believe people are drawn to those with similar narratives to themselves. This is above and beyond shared interests and beliefs. People who view themselves in similar ways can likely become good friends. Sharing a common view of self, as well as of the world through our values, can help us form bonds.

Commonality in self-narratives amongst friends can also be a way of reinforcing our narratives and keeping those narratives alive. As our self-narratives affect how we interact with others, we may amplify aspects of our narratives with others who share those aspects with us, further reinforcing and entrenching them.

This is certainly not a rule, and I didn't do any research to identify any patterns or verify this hypothesis, but thinking through people in my life, and observing other groups of friends, I think there is something to this. At the very least, this is something for you to consider as you reflect on your own relationships. Think about people in your life. Do they have similar self-narratives to you? Does this have an effect on your relationship with them? This doesn't have to be a bad thing, of course, and I would hope that mostly it wouldn't be negative. It can help you understand your own narrative as well as our relationships in new ways. It could also potentially allow you to see things about your friends that could help them. If someone is stuck with something or struggling with an aspect of their life and you're able to see a potential link to how they see themselves, you could potentially open them up to new ways of viewing themselves and moving beyond their struggles.

Perspective

Another key learning is that perspective is important, and this process has given me such a different perspective on pretty much every aspect of my life. Perspective allows us to put events into context instead of thinking solely about them in isolation. Often, things can seem like a huge deal, good or bad, when you are focused on them, but when you stop and think through them, they can turn out to be less important in relation to everything else going on in your life, or even in the world. Zooming out from the emotion and thinking about what is really going on helps, and having the awareness to stop yourself from obsessing over small things and thinking through your emotions is a valuable ability to develop.

I used to get very hung up on small things that happened, obsessing over details of events that really weren't important. It would be hard for me to let even little things go, instead just going over and over things in my mind. This interfered with my day-to-day life, my relationships, and my mental health as a whole. I have had struggles with anxiety over the years, and having my narrative influence my perspective or lack of fed easily into my anxiety-inducing thought processes.

So, how has understanding and redefining my self-narrative changed my perspective? With a better understanding of some of the causes of my emotions, I've been able to look at things with a new lens. I can now see that problems are often smaller than my emotions may lead me to believe. In fact, most of our day-to-day experiences are pretty insignificant in isolation, and it is not worth spending too much energy worrying about them or having them upset us. In my own life I can see this now. When my emotions creep up, instead of having them consume me, I'm now more inclined to try to understand them, and understand them in relation to everything else going on in my life. This is new for me, and it has helped me significantly. In short, having the ability to keep things in perspective, and having that greater view on my life has allowed me to chill out, and I'm much better for it.

7

How My Story Held Me Back

I've learned a lot through this process of self-reflection and growth, as I went through in the previous chapter. But what I'm going to share with you now is what has really been life-changing for me. I want to look specifically at the ways in which I have been held back. How I've been holding myself back, a hostage to my own narrative. This is the stuff that really started to make my life change.

Barriers

The biggest realization I've had is that our self-narratives can put up powerful barriers for ourselves. The story we tell ourselves about who we are, what we're capable of and our place in the world all influence what we do and don't do.

My self-narrative was holding me back. In my social life, I thought I couldn't connect to others so I didn't try, and at work I thought I wasn't really capable or as competent as others so I didn't speak up with my thoughts etc. These were barriers I had put up for myself. They weren't real, and they didn't have to be there. This was all me, and it was on me to do something about it, or continue to live in the suboptimal way I had been for the years of my early adulthood.

I started to see this, as I understood more about who I was, through self-reflection and a new openness to being honest with myself. It wasn't a quick realization, but I started to see glimpses of ways I was doing this to myself, and that just grew the more I reflected.

Once I realized I was being held back, I was able to try new things and take chances I wouldn't have before. Often these started with small baby steps, but slowly I would find out I was capable of doing things I never thought I could, and my confidence strengthened. The proof was there to see - the story I told myself that led me to believe I couldn't do something was a lie, and the evidence was right in front of me. The more I did this, the more I was able to push myself.

This is not to say that we are capable of impossible feats, and of course you have to be reasonable about the expectations you have. However, I believe understanding our own limitations is different to having artificial barriers that we put in place in our heads. I know, for example, that cannot work in sales. As I explored earlier, being an introvert doesn't mean I can't be outgoing, social and charming, but I still really need some downtime after such gregariousness as I can find this exhausting. Having a sales job doing this five days a week would be draining and ultimately damaging for me. I know this about myself, and I'm fine with it. But barriers I had about being social or not being able to fit in were things I put in place for myself and held me back from realizing what I was actually capable of.

Barriers that we establish for ourselves are tricky and powerful things. They are tricky because more often than not, you are not consciously aware that they are there. I always felt like it was just the way it was - for example, I thought I wasn't able to connect with anyone, and that translated to no close connections with people outside of my partner. This always bothered me, but slowly I started to see that this wasn't true. Honestly, it was a long process that took years, but I was able to slowly tear down this narrative and it opened me up to some new, strong connections with others.

Inaction

The barriers that I set up for myself not only led me to shy away from trying new things or speaking up and so on, but they also actually led to inaction in all sorts of other ways. There was of course inaction in trying to do things differently, but deeper than that, there was inaction on setting goals for myself. Because I believed my self-narrative, I didn't even think that I could achieve things so I didn't even aim to try. Even in areas of my life in which I was unhappy or wished were different, I was complacent or resigned to the idea that there was no alternative. And I certainly didn't strive for anything way out of my norm.

A perfect example of that is this book. As I began to explore this concept of our stories and how they influence us, I had the thought that I should write about it. I initially did - I published a personal essay and shared it online, got some amazing feedback and was incredibly proud of it. It gave me a high, being able to put something together and to hear how it resonated with others. At that point I knew I wanted to make it into a book. I knew it was important, that there was an audience for it, and that I could do it. But something got in my way. As I write this it's two years later, almost to the day, that I published that original essay online, and I'm finally doing it. And this is even after I started understanding about narratives and started to see my own barriers. A few years prior to this, just the mere thought that I could write a book would not have crossed my mind.

Self-narratives are not the only cause of inaction. Sometimes I'm just lazy. But it has been important for me to understand that some barriers I created for myself with my story led to me not setting goals and not trying new things, not being comfortable in whatever state I was in and not being willing to improve.

Self-Sabotage

This is bad stuff. I can't believe it's even a thing, but it is - I know because I've done it to myself, and only realized it long after the fact. The act of self-sabotage has to be the most treasonous thing imaginable. But it happens, over and over again.

Self-sabotage is a strong description of one of the most powerful ways our self-narratives impact our day-to-day lives. It is when we actually get in our own way and prevent ourselves from being successful. It can be about anything, big or small, but the important thing to note is that it is us doing it to ourselves. Why, you might ask, would we do that? Wouldn't we all want ourselves, as individuals, to be successful? Why would you prevent yourself from doing well?

I think the main reason this happens is when the change we are trying to make or the action we are trying to do goes against our self-narrative. The narrative we've told ourselves is so powerful, that when something happens that is counter to it, our subconscious pushes up against what we're trying to do. For me, I also think part of it is that I am afraid of change; it's generally very hard for me, so I try to resist it even when I am the one who initiates it. I also have realized looking back that, in some small way, I have been afraid of success. This makes no sense, I know. But this ties back to our narrative; being successful in something pushes against what I thought I was able to do, against that powerful narrative. Being successful has felt uncomfortable for me in the past, so there have been times I believe I have stood in my own way of achieving success because the status quo was way more natural for me.

Thinking through my own experience, I've identified

a number of ways in which I self-sabotage myself. The behaviours seem innocent enough, but they ultimately lead to creating barriers and prevent me from moving forward. This is how I believe it manifests for me. First, decision paralysis is a big one for me. When I need to make a decision to move forward, I get stuck in loops. Even for the smallest things, I stop myself from progressing by not being able to decide.

A second and related way I do this to myself is getting stuck in planning mode. Similar to decision paralysis, I can go over and over plans even when I know they are in a good state. I repeat, and analyze and over-analyze, when it is completely unnecessary. So, I spend my time planning and not doing. This happens often for me, and I can see now that it is in many cases a way that I self-sabotage.

The most common way I sabotage myself is probably by giving up easily. If I manage to get through the decision paralysis and planning loops and actually do something, I often find myself giving up at the first negative sign, or with the first resistance I encounter. Even after all the over-planning and time wasted thinking about it before doing anything, I am too able to throw in the towel upon receiving one negative signal. This is a problem I encounter a lot and I have had to fight myself to keep going when my natural instinct is to give up.

So, why can't we just not do this to ourselves? It happens in large part, I believe, because we are not even aware of it. For me, at least, these moments of self-sabotage happen without me being conscious of them.

I can see them in hindsight, but not in the moment. Never in the moment. This is what makes it hard to stop. It happens, as I mentioned, in large part because our self-narratives are so powerful and when you go against them you are going to meet resistance. And for me, staying the same or where I am is just so much more comfortable than something new, even if that new thing is personal growth or accomplishment.

So, what I've been doing instead of trying to stop it when it happens, is to instead work on what those root causes are, what my narrative is telling me. I've found this to be a much better strategy for me that ultimately has helped me reduce self-sabotage. Over the next chapters, I'll explore this more.

We Get in Our Own Way

To sum up this chapter, because of what the story I told myself was, I got in my own way. Constantly.

Barriers, missed opportunities, fear of failure, getting stuck in a rut. These are all things that get in the way of us achieving what we would ideally like to, or living our lives the way that would make us and those around us happiest. What's funny, or tragic, is that we can do this to ourselves. I learned this from my own experiences. We can be our own worst enemy, and be solely responsible for holding ourselves back. Often, instead of recognizing this and taking action to change, people complain or place blame on others. It can be easier to find faults in others or focus on how everyone else is preventing you from achieving your goals – whether true or imagined – than to look inward. But what we really need to do is stop expending energy on others and see how we are the ones holding ourselves back. And ultimately, then get out of our own way.

8

Self-Awareness

One of my biggest learnings is that self-awareness is crucial to understanding our self-narratives, and making any changes to them to improve our outlooks on who and where we are in life. None of what I talk about in this book - the learnings and gains that I've had – would be possible without self-awareness. This is such an important point that I'm giving it its own chapter. Self-awareness is where this all begins, and is how you can start to apply what I'm sharing in this book to your own life.

Before I go further, I will say that there are many resources on the topic of self-awareness, and if you want to really explore this concept then I encourage you to look into them. What I'm trying to do here is help you think a bit more about what self-awareness is and why it's important, and show you some basic ways that I've been able to develop my own self-awareness.

What Is Self-Awareness?

Googling "self-awareness" gives the definition as "conscious knowledge of one's own character, feelings, motives, and desires". Even as I type this in Microsoft Word, using the built-in thesaurus, the word awareness brings up consciousness and knowledge. So, self-awareness is all about being conscious and knowledgeable about ourselves, about our emotions and feelings, and our values and desires.

It may sound like something that is so obvious – how could we not be aware of these things? – but actually it is a skill that I've found I've had to focus on and develop to really realize the benefits. I know for myself, and for others that I've seen and talked to, it is so easy to go through our day-to-day lives without much thought to our emotions and behaviours, almost like we are on autopilot. Even when we experience strong emotions, many of us don't take the opportunity to fully explore what is really going on with us.

For me, being fairly sensitive and having emotions can consume me at times; being able to stop and think about what is actually happening and what it is about a situation that is making me feel that way has been one of the biggest things I've tried to do over the past few years, and it has had a tremendous impact for me. Understanding where my emotions come from doesn't make them go away, but it does make me able to respond to them in a more objective way.

So, why is it so hard then? It's not just being aware of

these things within ourselves, it's also truly understanding what is actually going on to then really know ourselves. Understanding who we are is something that I think we often don't give much thought to. Of course you know who you are, right? You're you! But do you know who you really are? This is where self-awareness comes in, starting to dig below the surface and finding out what we're really all about, our values, our beliefs, our stories about who we are. Without some deep reflection, I think it would be challenging for any of us to really know who we are. And without this deeper understanding of ourselves, we are closing off the potential for growth.

So, self-awareness is all about being aware of ourselves, our emotions, our thoughts. Easy, right? It's not as easy as it may seem, and I think for many of us it takes a lot of effort. The good news is that as I've found, self-awareness is something that we can put some energy towards and develop for ourselves.

Why Is It So Important?

I've established that self-awareness isn't always something that is natural to us. I've also mentioned that it is a skill that can be developed, but it isn't necessarily easy to do. So, is it worth the energy and effort to develop this further for yourself? Why is self-awareness so important?

Self-awareness is crucial to being able to improve ourselves. We need to have an understanding of who we are, how others see us, and what our opportunities for growth and change are before we can start to undertake any work to improve ourselves, or change situations and circumstances in our lives that we want to move away from or improve.

Our Place

Self-awareness can also help anchor us. It can be a way for us to understand and see our place in the world. Often, it's easy to feel lost in everything that is going on in our lives and the world around us. I know in the past I have felt lost, not knowing who I really was and how I fit into the world. This lack of direction and foundation prevented me from making decisions, being decisive and setting goals for myself. But by practising self-awareness, we can start to see how we fit in and be confident about who and where we are in our lives.

View of Ourselves

Another aspect is to understand how others see us. We might think we know how we come across to others, but without self-awareness, both internal and external (I'll get to that), we can have huge blind spots about ourselves and also about how we are perceived by others.

Without self-awareness, many of us have a skewed view of ourselves. Depending on what our narrative is telling us, we can overestimate or underestimate all aspects of ourselves – how smart we are, athletic, kind, efficient, productive, attractive. The list goes on. Our narrative influences our default position on these topics about how we are. Without some self-reflection and self-awareness, we can be very off from reality.

External Views

An important point that I just mentioned, that self-awareness has both internal and external components, is crucial to understand. The term self-awareness indicates that this has to do with us – looking internally to reflect and analyze ourselves. But you cannot be truly self-aware without also having an understanding of how you are perceived by the external world. Together, self-awareness gives you both insights into who you are and how you see yourself, and how the world sees you.

This is not something that may seem natural. For me, I was able to see the value of internal self-awareness. I could reflect and spend time internally understanding myself. But the idea of looking to others for feedback or commentary on me did not seem obvious, and actually felt very uncomfortable.

While it may not be natural to all of us, gaining understanding of how others perceive us, our actions and behaviours offers tremendous value as we try to understand ourselves and our self-narratives, and as we start to plan out changes we want to make in our lives.

Relationships

Self-awareness is also hugely important because it can have a tremendous impact on our relationships. How do your colleagues at work or your boss think of you, your behaviour, your communication? This can impact your career and professional relationships. Then, of course, our personal lives are affected by how others in our life see us.

If there is a disconnect between what our intentions are, how we think we are being seen and received by others and how they actually see us, this can be detrimental to our relationships, and hold us back across many aspects of our lives.

Self-Acceptance

Another aspect of self-awareness's importance in our lives, I believe, is to be around self-acceptance. Accepting who we are is easier for some than others. I myself struggled with many aspects of who I was, as I explored earlier in this book. But I found that through deep reflection, trying to understand my own narrative and practising self-awareness, I was able to not only get to know myself better, but to start to accept things that I originally saw as problematic. This process of self-awareness has allowed me to accept myself in ways I would have thought impossible even just a few years ago.

Enable Change

Finally, self-awareness is necessary to enable change. Really, all that this book is about, understanding the stories we tell ourselves about who and what we are, and trying to make improvements to ourselves, is not possible without self-awareness. It is the foundation of all of this.

In the next chapter I'll start by going into what I have done to understand my narrative and to identify things I wanted to change in my life, and the steps I outline are all, in some way, dependant on self-awareness. You cannot make meaningful, effective and sustained change without knowing who we really are.

How to Practise Self-Awareness

How can you develop or improve your own self-awareness?

The next section of this book is all about the process I went through to understand my own self-narrative and to look to change it. But, as I just mentioned, the foundation of all of this is really self-awareness. So, before we get to the next section, looking through the following pages will give you some insight into how to improve and develop your own self-awareness.

Be Open

One thing that is key to making this all work is that you keep an open mind. We have our self-narratives, beliefs about ourselves, things that we like and things that we don't like about who we are. But regardless of how power-ful that knowledge, or what we think we know about ourselves is (as we know, our self-narratives are powerful things!), keep an open mind, because you will probably start to learn things about yourself that are counter to what you thought you knew.

Do not let this discourage you, especially if what you find out is difficult for you to take. Just take it in. Don't judge it, don't judge yourself, that is not what this is about. Just let the learnings in, let them process, don't shut them out. This is important for you, so stick with it.

General Versus Situational

How do you actually start practising self-awareness? There are a couple of ways that I do it. The first is what I call "general" self-awareness. Basically, what this is is purposefully thinking about yourself.

This can happen in many forms, but it involves setting time aside to be with your thoughts, and thinking through your emotions or situations that happened to you.

For me, I started by just taking some time by myself in the evening to think about what happened during that day. What happened at work that went well? What didn't go well? How did I feel about it? I started to do this regularly, and it really started to help.

There were also times that people would say things to me or pose questions to me that would prompt me to reflect. For instance, I saw a therapist for a couple of years, and often he would post questions to me in our sessions that I would take away and start to think about. This led to some amazing realizations.

The second form of self-reflection I do is a little bit different. I call it "situational". I'm sure there are better names for this, but it works for me. This is more about when something happens that causes a reaction in me.

I'm sensitive and emotional so this happens often, where an event will happen or someone will say something to me that has an effect. In these moments, I start to break down the situation and ask myself what is really happening. I will explain the importance of such questions in the next section, but this is an important part of my self-reflection that not only helps in handling my responses to situations as they happen, but helps me take learnings from them right away.

The Right Questions

Questions are important, and often we don't ask ourselves the right ones. I've realized that often I jump to asking myself why in situations – Why did this happen? Why am I feeling like this? Why can't I do something no matter how hard I try? What I've come to realize is that beyond asking why I feel a particular way, often I don't really understand what is really going on. What is the situation that's happening, what is it really about?

This realization, surprisingly enough, came in part through my work. Working on quality improvement in health care, a big part is slowing down and understanding what the current state is. Thinking through what is actually happening to cause whatever we are responding to.

I started to learn that people are really quick to jump to solutions, without really understanding what the problem is. They may think they know what is happening, and what needs to be done, but time and time again I observed it wasn't actually what needed to happen to address the issue.

One of my biggest contributions at work has been to slow people down to start to ask questions that get to what is really happening, instead of just putting Band-Aid solutions on symptoms that are occurring.

This can be applied to our personal lives, too, and it has been a helpful tool that I've used to really understand what is going on.

Ask "What" instead of "Why". So, instead of asking yourself why am I feeling this way, think about it differently by asking what is actually happening right now. If you are feeling overwhelmed at the moment, instead of asking yourself why you are so overwhelmed, instead consider what is going on right now to make you feel overwhelmed. This will get to the conditions in the environment, or other factors that are leading to your response, and allow you to understand them better, and then plan changes to make improvements to your situation.

Ask Others

Going back to my point around internal and external self-awareness, it is crucial to gain an external perspective. This can be challenging, but it worth it.

Many of us do this in our professional lives already. We may have performance reviews at work, where we receive feedback from our manager and sometimes peers on how we perform and are at work, as well as identifying areas for improvement.

This can, and I think should, be done for our personal lives as well. You can do this by asking someone you are close to, like a partner or close friend who knows you well, for some feedback. It can be about specific areas you want to understand better – just ask them for their honest view. They likely see things about you that you don't and can provide really valuable information. Remember, keep an open mind and don't get mad at them for being honest!

Don't Get Stuck

As you go through this, it can be easy to get stuck in a pattern of analyzing and over-analyzing situations, asking yourself those "What has occurred?" questions. You do want to take a deep, honest view of what is happening, but do not let that be at the expense of actually planning and making improvements in your life.

Hopefully, you'll start to have some realizations and you can start to plan out how you can change things. It's important to be able to step back after a period of self-reflection and know what you've learned, and then be able to move on.

Patience

We live in such an instant society now, we expect results right away. But the thing about this stuff, what we're discussing here, is not a quick fix and can't provide instant results.

The bottom line is, you have to be patient. You can't expect to become fully self-aware today, and make all your changes happen tomorrow. People spend months, sometimes years, going through this stuff.

That's not to say that change can't begin to happen right away. When I had major realizations, it's like floodgates opened and all the opportunities suddenly seemed so clear to me. For me personally, though, some of those realizations only occurred after I was able to sit down with my reflections, almost like I was allowing my subconscious to process what I'd learned in order to let things surface. Be patient!

9

How to Do It

Here we are; you've heard my experience and what I've learned to be true for myself. You've learned about the importance of and how I practise self-awareness. Now what? If what you've read so far has resonated with you, then you might want to know what are the steps I took through this journey, and how you might be able to try a similar approach. While I didn't map it out like this as I went through these experiences myself, thinking through everything that has helped me, I've since identified and broken down my own process, which you can also try for yourself.

Before I begin, here's another disclaimer: What I've shared has been my personal experience, what I've learned about myself and how I have been able to use it. I am not sure this is truly a blueprint for how others can benefit from this process. We are all unique, have a diverse set of experiences and respond to them differently. What worked for me, and what I needed to focus attention on, may be different for you. And, of course, maybe you don't need to change, maybe your narrative holds true and isn't holding you back. And please note I certainly have no formal psychological training and this is only based on what I've done and what's worked for me. But at the very least, I think an act of self-reflection is a powerful and valuable one.

With that out of the way, there are a few key things that I think really helped me, though, and I would suggest these as starting points for you if you think you could benefit or feel like maybe your self-narrative is holding you back in some way.

First, I think it's important to mention a few things. You have to be honest with yourself. Really, really honest. This may seem obvious, but it is amazing how challenging this can be. Be open to this honesty, even when it's uncomfortable. If you don't, you won't be able to learn and grow.

This whole process was very uncomfortable for me. I was constantly challenging myself and my beliefs about myself and having inner battles against my own resistance to these challenges. It was really tempting to give up and it took a lot for me to keep going, to keep trying to see what I really wanted for myself and keep pushing forward. You might find this, too, and if so then please don't give up. It is always worth it to better understand yourself and push yourself to grow.

And please be patient. Changing your story takes time. It won't happen overnight. You are trying to undo years of a particular narrative. You have to repeat and let it set in over time, so stick with it.

Now, finally, here it is:

STEP 1: Know the Story You Tell Yourself

This is really what this book is all about. Know what your own self-narrative is, and try to understand how it has shaped who you are and how you interact with the world. This sounds simple – of course you know how you view yourself, right? You'd be surprised, as I was.

How can you do this? Start by just describing yourself. You can write it down if it helps. If you had to tell a stranger about yourself, what are the words that you would use? Don't overthink it at first, just note what immediately comes to mind.

Don't rush this. This is something that for me started to emerge over time; I started to slowly develop awareness of these different aspects and finally I was able to piece them together. Take some time thinking this through, and come back to it a bit later. More might come through as your subconscious works through it.

What came up? What were the positive things? Was there anything that was less positive or that you're less content with? Are there themes that you can see with how you describe yourself? These are important to take note of.

Also note the language that you use to describe yourself. You can dig into this later, as the words and your understanding of those words have importance to this whole process.

Thinking back to my story that I shared at the beginning of the book, I described myself as smart, a decent writer (hopefully you agree as you are reading this!), but I was shy, I had trouble connecting with others, didn't have close relationships, and thought people probably liked me because of my partner and not me. Being honest with myself, especially about the less desirable parts of my story, were really crucial for me to make any changes. Even the words I used, like "shy", had importance, as I explored earlier.

Note these things for yourself. Clarity comes when you know your narrative.

STEP 2: Ask Others What They Think

Part of my learning was that you can discover so much from how those who are close to you perceive you. It can be uncomfortable to ask, but those who know you really well will have a good sense of who you are based on your behaviours. Ask others, they can see things you can't.

For me, my story told me I was shy, and all the baggage that comes with that word. But those around me didn't see me that way. That was a truly mind-blowing revelation for me, and I was only able to have it because of that feedback from others.

STEP 3: Identify What You Want to Change

Now that you have a good handle on what your narrative is, as well as some outside perspectives, take some time and reflect on it. Does it feel like it fits? Are you happy with it? Are there things that you are unhappy with or you wish weren't part of how you view yourself?

Now think about how this has impacted on your life. Do you think this narrative has held you back in any way? Maybe not, maybe it all fits well for you and there's nothing obvious to change. That's great! But if there is something, that is what you can focus on. You have to be motivated to change it, otherwise it will be so easy to give up and return to your default.

For me, I wanted to change the thinking that I was shy and couldn't connect with others. I wanted to develop connections with others – that was one of the big parts of my story that I wanted to transform.

STEP 4: Imagine

If you've identified something that you would like to change or work on, the next step is to use your imagination. You want to change your thinking to what is possible instead of being stuck in compliance with the way things are.

For me, one thing that really stuck with me from therapy was when my therapist would ask me something to challenge my thinking and to get me to consider if a situation were different and for the better, he would say, "What would that look like?" I still often recall that, when thinking through how things could be different or how I could change things in my life.

The very exercise of envisioning what things could be like is actually really powerful. When we're so stuck in our narratives, it is hard to actually think about how things could be different. It's actually really difficult to do. But if you work your way through this process, and force yourself to think about how things could be different, it can open your eyes to what could be, and also highlight the ways in which your beliefs and narratives can hold you back.

One of my exercises around this that I went through with my therapist was around connections. He asked me what it would look like if I was able to really connect with someone new and make a strong friendship. The answer was hard to come up with because I really hadn't thought about what that would be like. But I talked it through and started to get an idea of what I could be, and what I wanted. It certainly wasn't a magic fix, but talking through this more and more with him and reflecting on it myself, I slowly started to believe that it could actually happen. And that belief was enough to enable me to start to view the world a bit differently, and this began to influence my actions. I started to see new opportunities for connections and to take action to try to build them. And, with time, it worked.

So, when thinking about part of your narrative that you want to change, think through what things could look like. Ask yourself what would it be to have a new narrative. And keep thinking about it, until you start to think it might actually be possible. You might find that, like me, this was enough to change your thinking, help you to be able to see new opportunities, and give you the motivation and encouragement to act on them.

STEP 5: Identify Your Barriers

A few chapters ago, I talked about my key learnings as I've gone through this process, and discussed some of the ways that my narrative held me back. The biggest way was that it put in place artificial barriers for me that prevented me from moving forward. These were my own creation, based on what my narrative was saying, and really didn't need to be there.

Think through what your barriers are. They might not be obvious, but it can help to think through what has prevented you from doing or acting the way you really wanted in the past. What got in your way?

Going back to my example, I thought I was shy so I didn't try to make connections with people. In reality, I was able to be social with the right conditions – when I realized this, I realized there was no reason for me to not try to make connections in other interactions with people. When I realized my narrative of being shy was a barrier, I was able to combat it and made so much progress.

When you know what your barriers are, you can try to stop them from getting in your way, or if they do come up you will be better prepared to know that they are there in the moment and try to remove them.

STEP 6: Stop the Negative Thinking

For some people this can be a big one. I know lots of people who get stuck with a negative outlook, are always complaining, blaming others. It can also be that voice in your head, your narrative self-sabotaging you. If this is true for you, STOP IT. Seriously, there's no use for this kind of thinking, it is just a huge waste of energy.

It can be hard to stop this, but it's important to recognize it when it is happening and to stop yourself. Practising self-awareness can help you be more aware of this.

The thing is, in life, sometimes bad things happen to us. They happen to all of us. We can't always control what happens to us, but, as the saying goes, we can control how we respond. This is so true. You can have an emotional response to something, which is fine and normal, but if it is negative, you should try to first of all see if there is a root cause to the response, as discussed in previous chapters, and work on changing your thoughts in the moment to ones that are constructive and forward-looking rather than dwelling on what went wrong or didn't go your way.

You can try to switch your mind into saying positive thoughts, even if you don't really believe them in the moment – in fact, it may feel like you are lying to yourself since you have likely become so used to and comfortable with negative thought patterns. But try to force it. Over time, this conscious effort will start to become unconscious and you will hopefully see those negative thoughts decrease.

STEP 7: Plan Your Action

You've identified your story, what you want to change and your barriers, and have worked on your negative thinking.

What now? As I discussed, you have to have actions that match your intentions. Things won't magically just change because you identify what you want to do differently.

You need to plan what you will do to move towards what you want to change. This can seem overwhelming and intimidating to even begin. I always find it helpful to think about the end result that I want, but then break it into smaller pieces. What would be something small that I can do now that is a bit different than what I have been doing?

If you are feeling overwhelmed, don't focus so much on the end result; this can seem so far from where you are today. Instead, think about what will help you get there? Are there people that you can talk to for advice, resources that you can read, actions that you can take? For me, trying to connect with others, I would start to talk to people at parties or social situations when before I would just be quiet. It wasn't always perfect, I had some awkward talks with people, but I tried it. And sometimes it worked.

Planning out your actions may seem hard, but part of this is changing your thought patterns. As you start to plan things out and hear the voice in your head say, "There's no way," fight that. Tell yourself, "I'm just going to try this and see what happens." This is the start of re-writing your self-narrative.

STEP 8: DO It

Now, do it! Really, this is the part where you need to take action. Take responsibility for your own life, your own growth and development. Just do it. Try.

I know this is easier said than done, but you just need to start. Try with something small, and see what happens. Don't get discouraged if you don't get the result you want. Try again or try something else. Eventually things will happen.

I found that I had to fight against my narrative; it was hard not to give up when things didn't go well when I tried something new. But I stuck with it, and eventually I started to see that things were changing. And seeing this is almost like a loop. It reinforced my plan for me, which made me want to keep going and try the next part of what I needed to do. This can really motivate you, so recognize the small things that go well.

When you actually start doing things you never thought you could, and getting some results that are really positive, your narrative will start to shift.

STEP 9: Self-Reflect the Entire Way Through

What the title says ^^^

And that's it. Nothing complicated. It's not of course a perfect roadmap but if you try it, I am hopeful that these steps and the self-reflection you undertake throughout will give you some great insights and a chance to make positive change for yourself.

10

A New Story

There **you have it.** I've shared with you what I've
learned and outlined the process that I have followed
for myself. Hopefully at this point I have given you
enough to think about in your own life and perhaps given
you a new perspective that can be beneficial.

We're at the end of what I have to share, so let's recap
what I think are the key things I've covered.

Big Takeaways

Some of the biggest learnings for me are here, and hopefully these are useful takeaways for you as well:

Stories Are Powerful

Stories and storytelling are incredibly powerful. We use

stories and storytelling to help with understanding and communicating, including having a story that we tell ourselves about who and what we are. This self-narrative is something we all have, and is deeply a part of what forms our identities.

Our self-narratives not only are a big part of our identities, but also influence our daily lives. This can be positive, but in some cases, they can actually hold us back.

Having our self-narrative tell us we can't do something or that we are just a certain way can mean we don't try to do things that don't fit this narrative. And this can close of so many opportunities and potential for us.

Our self-narratives are complex and deeply integrated into our subconscious. They originate from events and experiences in our childhood. Even little things that happened, things people said to us in passing, can have a huge impact in shaping our self-narratives.

Our stories are not static, though. As new experiences happen in our lives, our narratives can shift. Importantly, I believe that we can consciously change our self-narratives in helpful ways.

You Control Your Story

I've realized that we are the storytellers of our self-narratives and that we can control them. It's not easy but there are things you can do to challenge the beliefs you have about yourself through your self-narrative.

You are your own storyteller, and you can change your

own story. This can allow you to create positive change in your life.

Self-Awareness

None of this would be possible without self-awareness. Self-awareness isn't easy and doesn't come naturally for a lot of us. It's much easier for me to go through life without really thinking about what is actually happening, what my emotions and thoughts are really about. But the good news is that self-awareness is a skill that we can all develop. By practicing these skills, we are able to really understand what our feelings and thoughts are about, what the root causes of some of these things are and make changes to our self-narratives.

Changes

You can make changes to your self-narrative by first understanding it and understanding how it is preventing you from achieving what you want. How is it holding you back? Then think through what things could be like, imagine what is really possible. Stop the negative thinking. Plan out actions that you can take to move you beyond your barriers and towards what you really want. And do it. Repeat your new narrative if it helps. It will take a while to set in, but as you have a new narrative that allows you to do things you thought you couldn't, and as you actually start doing those things and then begin seeing the results, your self-narrative will start to shift.

My New Story

At the beginning of this book, I shared with you my original story. I talked about how I was awkward and had trouble connecting with others. And in my life at the time, this was true; I didn't try to connect with others because my story told me I couldn't. I was shy, and everything that that word implies. I didn't have many talents, and wasn't all that skilled or into interesting things.

I felt like I didn't fit in, and carried with me an incredible sense of "otherness" that made it hard for me not only to connect with others but also to feel like I had a place in this world. My story also told me I wasn't good enough in too many situations throughout my life.

After exploring these aspects of my narrative through the previous chapters, I am here now to share with you where I'm at. I've had a few years to develop an understanding of my self-narrative, where it came from and how it's held me back, and to work on changing it. I've come a long way and really have experienced so much personal growth through all of this. The change is not yet fully complete, and I still struggle with some old narratives creeping up from time to time, but overall it is working.

I'll leave you with the new story that I tell myself. A work in progress but one that is starting to stick:

I'm a nice guy, and am figuring out who I am. I value my personal time, and personal reflection, but enjoy being social and making connections with others. I'm smart and aware of the world around me, and can be interesting and engaging with others. I have some deep, meaningful connections with some very important people in my life, and am opening up to invite more of this kind of thing into my life. I'm learning what my talents are. I'm starting to see that I bring value to others and have ideas and thoughts worth sharing. I am learning to recognize where I struggle and how to find support. I'm learning, I'm growing, I'm changing.

I wish you the very best and know that you can use your self-narrative to make your dreams come true.

Bibliography

Ackerman, C. (2017, October 19). *The Big Five Personality Theory: The 5 Factor Model Explained (PDF)*. Retrieved January 01, 2018, from https://positivepsychologyprogram.com/big-five-personality-theory/

McAdams, D. P., & Mclean, K. C. (2013). *Narrative Identity. Current Directions in Psychological Science,22(3), 233-238.* doi:10.1177/0963721413475622

McAdams, D. P. (2013). *The Psychological Self as Actor, Agent, and Author. Perspectives on Psychological Science, 8(3), 272-295.* doi:10.1177/1745691612464657

McLean, K. C. (2008). *The Emergence of Narrative Identity. Social and Personality Psychology Compass,2(4), 1685-1702.* doi:10.1111/j.1751-9004.2008.00124.x

Moesgaard, S. (2017, June 23). *What is the Self and How is it Formed? 3 Very Different Theories Try to Explain it.* Retrieved January 01, 2018, from http://reflectd.co/2013/03/20/what-is-the-self/

Roberts, B., Luo, J., Briley, D., Chow, P., Su, R., & Hill, P. (2017). *Supplemental Material for A Systematic Review of Personality Trait Change Through Intervention. Psychological Bulletin. doi:10.1037/bul0000088.supp*

About The Author

Peter Ash is an independent writer from Toronto, Canada. He started writing as tool for self-reflection and personal development.

With some inspiration from creative friends, he wrote his first non-fiction book, *The Story I Tell Myself.*

Peter lives with his partner, Joshua, who continually inspires him to grow and learn. Peter's day job is in health-care administration, and he uses his writing for a creative outlet and to process his thoughts and reflections.

Connect

I hope you enjoyed reading this book and it gave you some new and interesting perspectives or thoughts on your own self-narrative. I invite you to connect with me, I'd love to hear what you thought and to stay in touch. You can find me:

http://www.peterwrites.ca/

Twitter:
@peterashwrites

Facebook:
https://www.facebook.com/peterashwrites/